# Aboriginal Legends of Canada

# Sioux

Megan
Cuthbert

Weigl

Published by Weigl Educational Publishers Limited
6325 10th Street SE
Calgary, Alberta  T2H 2Z9
Website: www.weigl.ca

Library and Archives Canada Cataloguing in Publication

Cuthbert, Megan, 1984-, author
    Sioux / Megan Cuthbert.

(Aboriginal legends of Canada)
Issued in print and electronic formats.
ISBN 978-1-77071-310-9 (bound).--ISBN 978-1-77071-311-6 (pbk.).--
ISBN 978-1-77071-312-3 (ebook)

    1. Dakota Indians--Folklore.  I. Title.
E99.D1C88 2013        j398.2089'975243        C2013-907332-9
                                              C2013-907333-7
Printed in the United States of America in North Mankato, Minnesota
1 2 3 4 5 6 7 8 9 0  18 17 16 15 14

062014
WEP301113

Photo Credits
Weigl acknowledges Getty Images and Alamy as its primary image suppliers for this title.

We acknowledge the financial support of the Government of Canada through the Canada Book Fund for our publishing activities.

Editors: Heather Kissock and Jared Siemens
Design: Mandy Christiansen
Illustrator: Martha Jablonski-Jones

# CONTENTS

# Meet the Sioux

The Sioux are one of Canada's **Aboriginal** groups. The Sioux divide themselves into one of three groups, called Dakota, Nakota, or Lakota Sioux. Together, these groups are known as the Great Sioux Nation. In the past, the Sioux moved often. They followed the bison, which were a main source of food and clothing for the people. The Sioux are originally from Manitoba, Saskatchewan, and the northern United States. Today, there are more than 12,500 Sioux living throughout Canada.

Storytelling has long played an important role in keeping the Sioux connected. In the past, the Sioux did not have a written alphabet. They passed on their history in several ways, from painting images on rocks to telling stories. **Elders** often gathered the young people around a fire to tell Sioux **legends**. These legends were a way to teach and entertain.

# Stories of Creation

One of the oldest Sioux stories is the story of creation. This story explains how the Sioux believe the world came to be. The Sioux believe a powerful being called the "Great Spirit" made Earth and all its creatures. The Great Spirit is a very important figure in Sioux creation legends.

The Sioux call the Great Spirit "Wakan Tanka," or "Taku Wakan." This name means "mysterious one" in their language.

One creation legend tells of a great flood that comes and covers the entire surface of Earth. It destroys almost every living thing. As people struggle to survive, they look to the Great Spirit for help. How the Great Spirit responds sets the course for the future of the Sioux people.

The Sioux often turned to the Great Spirit for help. They would ask for bountiful crops, safe travel, or protection from evil spirits.

In the past, the Sioux would gather inside teepees made of wood and bison hide to tell stories.

# Sioux Creation STORY

any years ago, a flood descended across the land. The waters rose as high as the nearby hills. The people tried to escape the rushing water, but they could not find a safe place. Just as the water began to sweep away the very last group of people, a beautiful woman in the group lifted her hands up to the sky. She begged the Great Spirit to save her from the flood.

The Great Spirit heard the woman's plea, and sent a giant eagle down to her. The eagle flew in close to the beautiful woman and grabbed her with its feet. Then, the eagle carried her to the safety of a tall tree on a high cliff. It was the only place the flood waters could not touch.

When the eagle landed, it turned into a man. The man and the woman married and had many children. One day, when the flood waters began to lower, the eagle took the woman and their children down from the tree. These children and their descendants became the Sioux people.

# Nature Stories

Nature was an important part of **traditional** Sioux life, and remains the subject of many Sioux legends. These stories help the Sioux describe how the land around them was shaped. Many Sioux nature legends explain why animals look or behave a certain way.

The Sioux relied on the **natural world** to provide them with food, shelter, clothing, tools, and medicine. They made sure to treat the animals with great respect. The Sioux developed strong bonds with these animals. *The Pact of the Fire* shows how the Sioux and the dog came to be good friends, and how each helps the other.

Before horses were introduced to North America, the Sioux used dogs to help carry their belongings.

Bison were a main source of food for the Sioux. The Sioux also made tools from the parts of the bison that could not be eaten.

# The PACT of the FIRE

After the world was created, First Man and First Woman struggled to survive the winter.

First Dog was also struggling. First Dog gave birth to a litter of puppies. The puppies became hungry, but First Dog could not find food for the puppies and keep them warm at the same time.

The winter was so cold that First Dog was afraid the puppies would freeze without her warmth. As she huddled in the brush of the forest, she could see the fire that First Man and First Woman used to warm themselves. Before too long, she had no choice. She was starving and would soon die.

First Dog went over to First Man and First Woman and asked them to make a deal. If they would feed and raise her puppies, the puppies would guard the camp and warn them of danger. First Man and First Woman agreed to the deal. Since then, dogs have been loyal friends to humans.

# Life Lessons

Storytelling helps the Sioux to teach their children important values and beliefs. In the past, Sioux elders were responsible for telling these stories to the youth. Many of these stories teach children how to behave and treat one another. The stories often show what happens when people do not behave in a proper manner.

In the past, the Sioux sometimes told stories using a form of sign language. Hand gestures and movement helped tell the story to Sioux groups who spoke a different language.

The Sioux relied on hunting and gathering for most of their food. However, finding food could not be taken for granted. Weather, such as hail or frost, could destroy plants. People also competed with animals for the same foods. *The Forgotten Ear of Corn* helps to explain why it is important not to waste food.

Long ago, the Sioux painted life lessons and historical events on animal hides. These hides, called winter counts, help preserve Sioux history.

Dancing is one of several ways that the Sioux share stories with one another.

# The FORGOTTEN Ear of CORN

A woman was gathering corn from the field for winter. As she went through the cornfield, picking corn from the stalks, she heard the faint sound of a child weeping.

"Do not leave me! Do not go away without me," the voice said. The woman searched for the voice in the cornfield but could not find the crying child.

As she went to leave, she heard the child's voice again. After searching for a long time, she finally found a small ear of corn beneath the fallen leaves of the cornstalks. It was crying because all of the other corn was being taken away. It was afraid that it would be left behind and forgotten.

It said the Great Spirit wanted people to be more careful with their crops. The people must not waste any food. This would make the Great Spirit unhappy like the forgotten corn.

# Heroic Tales

**M**any Sioux legends feature characters who behave with **honour** and courage. These characters display the **traits** the Sioux admire. They are able to use their **intelligence** and skill to solve problems and help people. The characters teach Sioux children about the importance of bravery, strength, and wisdom. They set an example for others to follow.

Often, heroes will go on journeys and encounter difficulties they have to overcome. *The Legend of Stone Boy* tells the story of a Sioux hero who tries to find his missing family members. Stone Boy has to use his strength and **perseverance** to help find his family and bring them home.

According to one Sioux legend, Stone Boy was born after his mother swallowed a smooth white stone.

Sitting Bull was a Sioux chief and a hero of his people. His fearlessness made him a fierce enemy in battle.

# The LEGEND of STONE BOY

There once was a girl who lived with her five brothers. She spent her day cooking and making clothes while her brothers went hunting. One day, only four of the brothers came back. The next day, the four brothers went hunting, but only three returned. This continued each day until the girl's last brother did not return.

The girl was so upset that she swallowed a stone. A few months later, she gave birth to a boy made of stone. She named him Stone Boy. Stone Boy grew quickly. When he was a man, he went on a journey to find his uncles. He came across an evil old woman who tried to poison him. Stone Boy did not die because he was made of stone. He found five bundles in her teepee that contained the remains of his uncles. Stone Boy pressed the old woman until she told him how to bring his uncles back to life. Stone Boy did what she said, and his uncles appeared before him. Then, Stone Boy and his uncles returned home.

# Activity

## Make a Winter Count

The Sioux sometimes used winter counts to record their stories. Follow the instructions below to record an important event in your life on your very own winter count.

### You will need:

Scissors

White glue

Felt markers, paints, pencils, or crayons

One piece of beige coloured craft paper, felt, suede, or canvas

### Directions:

1. Cut a shape out of the fabric or paper.

2. Think about the best day that you have ever had. Who was there? What happened? How did you feel?

3. Think of one picture or **symbol** to represent each question above for your winter count.

4. Create your symbols by drawing them on the fabric or paper. Or, draw symbols on other fabric, cut them out, and glue them onto the fabric or paper.

5. When your winter count is complete, tell your friends and family the story of your best day using each of the pictures.

# Further Research

Many books and websites provide information on Aboriginal legends. To learn more about this topic, borrow books from the library, or search the internet.

## Books

Most libraries have computers that connect to a database for researching information. If you input a key word, you will be provided with a list of books in the library that contain information on that topic. Nonfiction books are arranged numerically, using their call number. Fiction books are organized alphabetically by the author's last name.

## Websites

Learn more about Canada's Sioux at esask.uregina.ca/entry/dakota_lakota.html

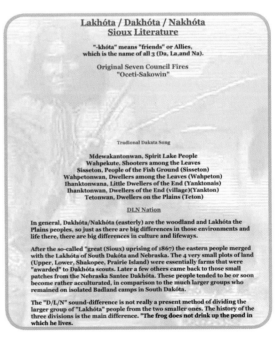

Read different Sioux legends at www.indigenouspeople.net/sioux.htm

# Key Words

**Aboriginal:** First Nations, Inuit and Métis of Canada

**elders:** the wise people of a community

**honour:** a sense of what is right or honest

**intelligence:** the ability to think, learn, and understand

**legends:** stories that have been passed down from generation to generation

**natural world:** relating to things that have not been made by people

**perseverance:** the ability to stick to a purpose or aim

**symbol:** something that represents something else

**traditional:** based on established practices and beliefs

**traits:** qualities or characteristics

# Index